THE BROKEN FLOWER

THE BROKEN FLOWER

JEFFERY BEAM

SKYSILL PRESS

Copyright © Jeffery Beam 2012

The right of Jeffery Beam to be indentified as the author has been asserted by him in accordance with Section 77 of the Copyrights, Designs, and Patents Act 1988

All rights reserved

ISBN 978-1-907489-13-6

Cover image: Mirror, Museo Vetrario (Museum of Glass), Murano, Venezia, September 2011

© Elizabeth Matheson 2012

SKYSILL PRESS
3 Gervase Gardens
Clifton Village
Nottingham   NG11 8LZ

skysillpress.blogspot.com

For Cindy Adams, Sue Anderson, Susan Arnold, Catalina Arocena, Daphne Athas, Cynthia Baker, Nancy Baker, Ann Barlow, Kate Barnhart, Milly Barranger, Lois Bateson, Jessica Bayer, the late Anne Beere, Libba Beerman, "Mrs. Benfield", Maudy Benz, Sandy Black, Ginger Blunden, the late Elizabeth Bolton, D. J. Bost, Margie Bost, Jennifer Brown, Mary Finch Bullock, the late Mary Jane Burns, Libby Chenault, Karen Ciccone, Jill Coleman, Nicole Condoret, Donnetta Cook, Gail Cooley, Deborah Coram, Alice Cotton, "Mama Dip" Council, Cynthia Cowan, Perry Craven, the late Anna Darden, Donna Dickinson, Karen Dillon, Pat Dominquez, the late Hilda Doolittle, Linda Drake, Shirley Drechsel, Kim Duckett, Elizabeth Dunn, the late Didi Dunphey, Barb Duvall, Emma Duvall, Erica Eisdorfer, Alice Faulkner, Elena Feinstein, Besty Fenhagen, Sue Field, Patricia Finch, Debbie Finn, Keebe Fitch, Penelope Foster, Mimi Fountain, Susan Frankenberg, Laura Frankstone, Nancy Frazier, Rachel Frew, Lynn Friede, Doris Friend, Astrid Furnival, the late Maud Gatewood, Pilar Gizzi, Louise Glück, Nancy Goodwin, Frances Gravely, Margaret Grayson, Libby Grey, Marilyn Gunn, Wanda Gunther, Brigitte Hamilton, Ann Hamrick, the late Bertha Harris, Anna Hayes, Nancy Heath, Ellen Hemphill, Mimi Herman, Mary Hill, Maggie Hite, Dot Hodges, Jane Holding, Lyn Holdzkom, Shauna Holiman, Geneva Holliday, Deb Hollis, Bonnie Holt, Vicky Beam Holt, Susan Holt, Susan Inglis, the late Alice Ingram, Linda Jacobson, Martha Jenkins, Karen Jessee, Amy Johnson, Helen Johnson, Debra Kaufman, Miriam Kennard, Erin Kimrey, Harriet King, Ellie Kinnard, Betsy Klenowski, Barbara Kremen, the late Georgia Kyser, Lucy Finch Lamm, Louise Landes-Levi, Pat Langelier, Jeanette LeBouef-Kassam, Janet Lembke, Doris Lessing, the late Denise Levertov, the late Edna Lewis, "Mrs. Lippard", Sheila Lund, Heather Main, Tricia Maloney, Muriel Mandel, Harriet Martin, Sally Massengale, Elizabeth Matheson, Nancy Tuttle May, A. J. Mayhew, Margaret McAdams, Catherine McCrae, Ann McGarrell, Margaret McKimmon, the late Betty Meehan-Black, Eva Metzger, Coolie Monroe, Andrea Moore, the late Hilda Morley, Mary Morrow, Jennifer Moye, Patricia Moyer, Jill Muti, Florence Nash, Maragarite Nathe, Madeline Neal, Moreton Neal, Catherine Nicholson, the late Lorine Niedecker, the late Anaïs Nin, Ellen O'Brien, Jane Oldham, Mary Oliver, Kristin

Olson, Andrea Owens, Angie Owens, Cristi Owens, Maria Owens, Patricia Owens, Jenny Owens-Shaw, Bess Oxendine, Jan Paris, Ella Parsons, Ippy Patterson, Maria Petruz, the late Sylvia Plath, Celia Pratt, Sudie Rakusin, Leigh Raynor, Sandra Reese, "Mrs. Reid", Molly Renda, the late M. C. Richards, Leonora Rogers, Franca Rustioni, Sharon "Pinkie" Ryan, Margaret Sartor, Alison Schroeer, Sarah Schroth, the late Nellie Sellers, M. J. Sharp, Blaisdell Shaw, Jill Shires, Rita Shumaker, Ann Skelly, Delacey Skinner, Margaret Skinner, Sue Slatkoff, Kim Sloan, Stacie Smith, the late Stevie Smith, Jen Snider, Elizabeth Spencer, Christine Stachowicz, Diane Steinhaus, Ci Ci Stevens, Ann Stewart, Martha Stewart, Diana Stoll, Ronnie Moon Stone, Danielle Strauss, Diane Strauss, Elena Strauss, Martha Strawn, Charlene Swansea, Liza Terll, Lucinda Thompson, Pat Thompson, the late Daisy Thorp, Laurie Thorp, Patti Thorp, Ginger Travis, Lynn Turner, Erica Van Horn, Charlotte Vestal, Mary Frances Vogler, Rebekah Wade, the late Phyllis Walsh, Alice Welsh, Mahnaz Whelton, Alice Whiteside, Susan Whitfield, the late Collin Wilcox-Paxton, the late Georgette Williams, Julia Willis, Anabelle Clare Wilson, Elizabeth Woodman, Liz Woodman, Pat Woods Belden, Drena Worth, Claire Yaffa, Margaretta Yarborough, Marly Youmans, and "Ms. Zipper".

In memory of
My mother, Allie Mae Ervin Beam
My grandmother, Willie Mae Gill
My grandmother, Scottie Marie Ervin

And in honor of
My "mother-in-law" Bonnie Finch

The Goddess Incarnate.

Without beauty, what would become of being?
Without being, what would become of beauty?

—Plotinus

CONTENTS

A POEM OF PREFACE

Last Born   3

THE WAY IT HAPPENED

The Way it Happened	7
The Clouds	8
Credo	10
On a Japanese Woodcut: Woman Looking in a Mirror	12
Bobwhite	15
Vase of Dried Poppies and Dock	17
Luminist Landscape: Scaly Mountain	19
Snake in Autumn	20
Walking on Apples	21
This Journey	22
Coming Home	23
The Flies	24
The Other	25
A Birthday Valentine: *Althea rosea*	27
The Room of the Poet	29
The Sunflowers	30
What We Find There	31
In Praise of Shadows	32
The Dog as Healer, The Snake as Cure	34
John the Baptist	35
St. Eustace	37
The Seeker	38
A Stone Falling, A Falling Stone	40
The Broken Flower	41
Oh, and I Thought	43
The Suicide	45
Against Sorrow	46
The Explorer	48

Paracelsus: Concerning the Iris in the Vase	50
Toil, a Divine Commandment	51
The Man Who Ate Butterflies	52
The Poppy Suite	53
July Apples	56
October Song	58
The Raising of Lazarus	59
The Dream	61
I Have Never Wanted	62

WINTER CEDARS

Ghazal of Lament	67
Meditation on the Death of a Bird	68
Le Quattro Stagioni	69
Spring, Summer, Fall, Winter	
Monet	73
The Loom	74
The Stroke	75
Owl Flight	77
The Crab King	78
Moss	80
Albino Deer	81
On Watching a Storm Approach	83
Fog	84
Rising	85
A Spell for Poem Making	86
The East	87
A New Usefulness	88
Cityscape	89
From a Train at Dusk Somewhere in Virginia	91
Persimmon	92
A Pause for Celebration	93
Alzarsi col sole	94

Natty Kathmandu Dreads	96
Kali	98
Scorpion	99
Shadow	100
Dog Sleeping	101
Cat Poetry	102
In Provence	104
Lunch	105
In Lucca	106
Parnassus, the Barren Cleft	107
Winter Cedars	109

POSTSCRIPT

Teaching Daylilies How to Read	111

THE BROKEN FLOWER

All bliss
Consists in this,
To do as Adam did.

—Thomas Traherne

A POEM OF PREFACE

Things are not only what they are. They ceaselessly pass beyond themselves and give more than they have. They are better and worse than themselves, because being superabounds, and because nothingness attracts what comes from nothingness.

—Jacques Maritain

When the artist rose high enough to achieve the beautiful, the symbol by which he made it perceptible to mortal senses became of little value in his eyes while his spirit possessed itself in the enjoyment of the reality.

—Nathaniel Hawthorne

LAST BORN

The sack she prepared
burst under a great weight of bone
I began to sift through pebbles
for my name

THE WAY IT HAPPENED

I would call back ... this world of shadows we are losing. In the mansion called literature, I would have the eaves drop and the walls dark. I would push back into the shadows the things that come forward too clearly. I would strip away the useless decoration.

—Junichiro Tanizaki

For in the immediate world, everything is to be discerned, for him who can discern it, and centrally and simply, without either dissection into science, or digestion into art, but with the whole consciousness, seeking to perceive it as it stands; so that the aspect of a street in sunlight can roar in the heart of itself as a symphony, perhaps as no symphony can: and all of consciousness is shifted from the imagined, the revisive, to the effort to perceive simply the cruel radiance of what is.

—James Agee

THE WAY IT HAPPENED

It began on the roof
He took a broom up the ladder
Started sweeping the debris of three autumns
The wind sound the Dead
removing make-up from their faces
He swept until bugs under pine needles
rode their wings skyward
He a baby
in a crib crying facedown into pillow demons
This poem a black shape
breathing in the straw

THE CLOUDS: GREAT SMOKIES

Here
the nights are
mostly foggy

though at times
the sky clears
and

you can see
the moon,
stars, and

the end
of the universe
glistening—

a silver spoon.
Mostly though
in late summer

it is fog,
mist,
the moon peeks out

Victorian and
saintly.
On this mountain

the clouds
come down
to sit

for their supper.
Late night:
no dinner

or dancing.
Just a simple
sleep

among ash and
hickory.
A coverlet

for birds.
A welcome
sinister

necklace
for men
and dogs.

CREDO

Now, when I talk
it is not just to say
this or
that.
But it is to say
what is between.

Over there,
under the sycamore, runs
the argumentative
periwinkle.
The blue eye
of southern spring.

Over there,
chickadee whistle
and blue
bird.

Here swings
the blues'
rightful cadence.
Words melancholic
swarm, thick with
dribble, and
slang.

To my own self
be true.

To say what is
between:
the periwinkle,
the chickadee.

ON A JAPANESE WOODCUT: WOMAN LOOKING IN A MIRROR

After Kitiagwa Utamaro

I.

What he sees
in the mirror
is not himself, but
another's image,
lost
looking.

What she sees
in the mirror
is herself,
a Japanese
matron claimed by
pear blossom,
sweet cinnamon.

What he sees in the woodcut
is her seeing,
then,
himself,
again in his mirror.
How like her
he seems.

Nothing is as dark as
he thinks.
The light reflected shapes
thoughts
refracted.

When the mirror reveals him,
a dark man
in a dark time,
with light
shining behind,

he feels the woodcutter
carefully
molding
her face.

2.

Oh. So that is what you think?
Tonight stars whirl

in their caves—
eyes sink
to the pool of withering
morning glories.

*Are these my hands, the clink
of silver bracelets, mine?
The silken shawl
fallen at the shoulder?
Is that mine, too?*

*Last night,
among the men,
I left a smoky wave
gathering outside.
I looked.
In the bridge's shadows
I saw,
the cranes.*

*Take me home, brother.
Winter leaves a feathery sound
blackening my lips.
Tonight I would sleep
under the rain tree's branches,
in a bed
of dry water,
below this*

mottled starry cave.

BOBWHITE

At midday they come,
                wary and solid.
                              The male in his striped

white
        hood,
                the female,

fawn and alert,
                marching their Egyptian lunge
                          three hundred

yards from
        thicket
                to feeder.

Cats inside,
        sleeping and unaware.
                Dog inside,

sleeping and caring less.
        The downy pecker,
                doves, finches

chickadees, juncos,
        a moving chiaroscuro.

                                        Come the quail.

Painted,
                    pointillist,
                                        artful.

Sincere.
                    Quiet.
                                        While all come

and go.
                    When all is safe
                                        and cool.

In winter damp.
                    In cloudy
                                        light.

VASE OF DRIED
POPPIES AND DOCK

The wildness of it
is what's so circumspect.

That at any moment
the pure colorless

dullness,
its wild

form,
might break

ranks and show
unabashedly

what it had been:
red opium and

rank weed.
Cow pasture and

foreign lands.
Civilization's history

in raw color.
Uninhibited now

by that,
it fills the vase

and my eyes,
declarative and

unashamed.
Naked

as a newborn babe.

LUMINIST LANDSCAPE: SCALY MOUNTAIN

The pileated wood
                pecker
  calls
     from insanity's tree,
brash and
              ephemeral as
the jewel weed...
Roadside merlins:
                mist
         and
                fog.
Dead logs, moss
                  encrusted
at evening's water
                fall.

SNAKE IN AUTUMN

I could have stood there
                                  until
            the creek dried up.
Coiling
            and uncoiling. I
was that happy and that
                              terrified.

        The snake is silent.

The coiling and uncoiling.
                              Silent.
Both blessed and troubled—
                           I
radiant in my
                red and blue heats
                before him.

The yellow came from him.
                    A golden mesmerizing eye.
Between us
            the creek flowing.
Coiling and un-
                coiling.

WALKING ON APPLES

You think you know how it will be
smooth and crunchy unlike
a brain
Without ecstasy and with
much derision
the dull
thuds dropping
round you in the tall
grass   The bees
serenade

Instead
a lemon odor
from the dying bellies
A narrow track trampled
in the grass
leading to the woods
up which nightly
a solitary small beast comes
to take with hunger
and no greed
the rounded vapors left by wasp
and beetle

THIS JOURNEY

This is a good place
You have come without anything
but the smell
                  on your hands
of your suitcase from a previous journey

Perhaps a word   or two
spoken in
                another language
perhaps
                one songbird's tender
mercy under a summer sun

It is a good place   surely
for you are
                here
without malice
                and if   as you think
it must be true:

there is a reason for being here
        whatever it might be
                however
it insinuates itself into you

COMING HOME

Street lights come on.

Not dark
yet,
        but tree-frogs open
their symphonic bags to begin tuning.

When the hooded one stands behind you
tapping his foot to the music
you know you are chosen.
                        He opens the book.
Shows
        you the emblem.
That birth mark on your back.

Suddenly,
                you see everything
                behind you.

THE FLIES

They visit a country where flesh is only a language. A country of wide vistas, brown prairies, where air currents are impassioned, young and unencumbered. They have prepared for this carefully, remembering their ancestors, some wingless, who became anonymous as milk. They prepare to never again be anonymous. Somewhere their hungry secrets accumulate, debtless, waiting for a signal from below.

Our destiny is to witness. The first place we are taken is familiar, the small pain from a needle. Lessening our will, they invade, pouring sulfur into the windows. This is the original country. The fluid nation. Beyond boundaries. The Flies pinch and sting. Their anger knows no solace. They dress in green and purple robes. Afterwards, the sun sets. The moon comes out, thread in the undergarments of the drowned.

In a fortnight, the Flies are gone. We discover their final instructions: a few detached wings, crushed antennas, a green puddle of inner antagonisms. We wonder at their brevity, whether their soul's wit is as delicate as ours, and whether we will follow. We visit a country where flesh is known only as language. A country of narrow stone streets, windless and stale. Some of us, wingless, accumulate hungry secrets. We wait for a signal from above.

THE OTHER

When the spirits come out of a fleshy tunic that is a dead body (said Belibaste, one of the villagers interrogated), they run very fast for they are fearful. They run so fast that if a spirit came out of a dead body in Valencia and had to go into another living body in the Comte de Foix, if it was raining hard scarcely three drops of rain would touch it! Running like this, the terrified spirit hurls itself into the first hole it finds free! In other words into the womb of some animal which has just conceived an embryo not yet supplied with a soul; whether a bitch, a female rabbit or a mare. Or even in the womb of a woman.

From *Montaillou: The Promised Land of Error* by Le Roy Ladurie.
Words spoken by the Cathar Perfect Belibaste

After this we start back alone
sure that the spirit has begun
its wandering
                          wondering where
   on this bleak night
                                after this
        after stars have fallen
        and the spirit of this place
        has forsaken its habitual tunic.

The spirit runs fast
                    fearful
  runs fast
                    quaking at the strangeness
                                      without
  scarcely touched by
                    the niagara soaking
                    its flimsy loins

What, to die?
                        This? Hurry, fast
  Oh, I am terrified!
                                   hurling
      itself at the first free embryo
into a new name
                        and conception.

I cannot bear the space
                        the wideness amazing
           in its vacuum—
take me into a body.
                            And the sleeve
        drops down quick over
                            the buzzing centrifuge
   found.

In the town
        under steel-blue moans
        the fire's warmth
        the newly welcomed
        wallows in sweet linen rolls

    with candles lit
    for the dear
              departed.

A BIRTHDAY VALENTINE: *ALTHEA ROSEA*

For Stanley, April 4 and 5, 1992

Would that in this
                early April of our births
                              the hollyhock, out-
landish rose of the Crusaders,
                might guard the garden walk,
                        in bloom.
Too early for that, but
                not for the curled mound
                            of rich green leaves
precious as their Chinese
                and Indian origins.
                            While the bees sleep
so
                do these flowers.

Love comes out
                of nowhere, or anywhere,
                          or every,
And so,
                like these mallows,
                            warm underground
through Winter's wet mess and slump:
                my love always.

                                          For summer hides
continually in the leaves,
                    and at once,
                                      when the sun calls,
opens pink and
                  singular on the stiff
                                stalk.

THE ROOM OF THE POET

is like no other room
These gold-beaked birds
sip on remnants of fish
Candles freeze with words
opaque and blue
Armpits glisten with saliva
Fingers remove garments
from the spirit
One by
one

THE SUNFLOWERS

All about me people
mingle in and out among the bodies
of themselves and the selves
of others. I wonder how they go
about their business without collapsing,
without their bones breaking
under the knowledge that all
things change. They surprise me
as they move and intertwine
and disintegrate. Something
holds them up. Some glue.
Or miracle. My other tells me
of Faith, the striving
to Perfection leading us.
How together
we will be made
new.
Above,
a sparrow sings with
the tall flowers.

WHAT WE FIND THERE

Darkness in the cupboard's corner.
Kitchen warm with baking bread.
In jars: beans,
grains.
Take the simple dark as a robe.
Fire, lit.
Pot, steaming.

IN PRAISE OF SHADOWS

People say
                      we should not linger
with grief
                      but bind
instead the bruise
with the future's
                      sweet petals

I can't deny that grief's
tentacles
are marine
                      carnivorous
but
          in deepest oceans
                          fish
variegate their own lanterns

The amaryllis
                    a flower
I have called before
takes to the dark
with vengeance
                    multiplying
scarlet trumpets
when the sun
fills
          finally the kitchen

My God, we leave
behind so much
to gain a little

When
           to go forward
we should only have to
                              strike
      a stone for fire
in the wine
cool darkness

THE DOG AS HEALER THE SNAKE AS CURE:
A Healing Poem

For Tunney Cobb

*And there are records of many cures
effected by the healing tongues of both
dogs and serpents during the incubation
of those who came praying for healing.*

Maria Leach, *God Had a Dog*

Fear nothing, no matter
what. In your sleep, that perilous
place, will come
dogs and serpents licking
with their tongues.
Ointments will be spread,
foul odors and sharp pain
diminished. Wounds healed
miraculously. Sorrows erased.
The narrow hairy face
of man's best friend, your
four-legged mentor, will
embrace you. The serpent
in your belly will laugh.
Fear nothing, no matter
what. It has been
this way
forever.
And will be
again.

JOHN THE BAPTIST

The one who comes from above
Is over all
He who is earthly
Belongs to the earth
and speaks to the earth

Gospel of John, translated by Kalmia Bittleson

In Andrea del Sarto's painting of Saint John,
the voice crying from the wilderness
is soft and pliant, wreathed by
ivy in the hair—a natural halo.
John's a rugged youth,
splendidly smooth and hard,
draped royally in holy red and brown.
One finger and thumb
from the right hand
point heavenward and to the humble,
thin cross of sticks he carries
for a staff.
Already the fire of Grace
illuminates his face. And the coarse
curls surround him wildly,
umbrous and jungled.
Why does he, then, look down if
not to gaze at earth's lovely darkness
and the water's clean rinse?

For as he points upward, looking
down, the whole story
is told.
The light shining in the darkness, and
the darkness
which cannot hold.

ST. EUSTACE

After Dürer

  But you come anyway, not that I want you, nor even care. For something in the day's search, the hunt, has led me to you. Summer fills my boots with sweat, my green felt hat tarnishes in the sun, and for a fortnight before, my nights have railed with grave forebodings, demons and ponderous laurel.

  There you are. The stag. Bearing your cross. Those impregnable horns. The woods sweet with buckthorn and ash, suddenly, as after spring rain moss audibly grows. My horse mirrors your gaze, and my hounds bate as before a hearth. I see myself in you and all the red battles I have led. Nowhere have I known such peace … even among the Dead of whom I know so many … those cold hands and spirits ringing variable tones by the shaking of their shrouds.

  Could I but smell a fiery oven, I would plunge into it. Happily.

THE SEEKER

For Anna Hayes

How long have I been without an answer.

For now,
        I am without one

needing a new acoustic,
                much time
                keeping silent.

The deer leap through tall grass:
                landlocked dolphins.
The golden empire of the grass.
The deer's telegraphic warning.

As Rilke said:
            perhaps "mere being
can become an event
                for us"
so that
        we do not have to move toward it

but through it

(as the deer).

Like the others, I am full
                    as pomegranates
lavishing my rich clay
                    upon the tongue.

Such good odor and miracles
                    bright as flowered bed covers
must await us.

                    But where
the purest air?

With closed eyes we can feel
                    the clouds.
We are all waters,
all unfoldment and melody,
                    stars
revolving in frigid air.

Rilke again:

"We simply *don't know*
what need destroys in a heart,

what it erects."

A STONE FALLING,
A FALLING STONE

I am not afraid to fall.
Drop me from a tower and I
simply hit the earth. Hold on
to me, I am earth still.
I want to fall, it is the first
dream for me. And the earth
my drum that I play.

A stone falling, a falling stone.
Whether I burn or not—
that's beside the point.
The point, this:
when the earth
makes a stone
the sky still fathers it.
When the earth makes a stone,
it's made for falling.

I am not afraid to fall.

THE BROKEN FLOWER

For Alexander Gilmore III

That a broken flower
could speak or

a bird's feather
found forlornly on the path

tell symbols
amazes us.

The last place we would think
to look

there in the discarded
shattered world.

The petals no
less lovely still sing

a loving intention.
The feather a floating

memory forever lightened
by its past.

The hand which carries them
the way humans can

when that which is broken or
displaced is made repaired,

renewed. Rediscovered:
the most perfect flower the most

perfect feather.
That the flower

has no stem only
confirms it.

OH, AND I THOUGHT

1.

Oh, and I thought I was special.
It's a game we humans play
to attract your attention. We
think that persistence in
believing it is all for *us*, separately,
will make you come down, cover us like
snow, each chosen, quietly, before the doom
of Death, that close darkness,
takes us up, and Death instead
will be white shadows, and
cold, simple, silence. Instead,
we are meant to learn its
opposite. All together we *are*
special, but separately, *never*.
Spokes in an eternal wheel.

2.

I lied before when I said
separately we're not special.
A half-truth at least. Both,
neither/and, we are conflict
impossible to define without
exaggeration or egotism.
In and out of the world
our roles differ, but when
in the world most fully, but

simultaneously, aside, a vibration
begins. A tree bends. The
wind through our branches.
Then. That's the special time.

THE SUICIDE

After Rilke's letters

The open lake,
indescribably open to all.
The dismal background.
This lovely prospect.

Nearly astonished,
I have been ready
to renounce
all its blessings.

Nature, if I am not yet
entirely lost to you:
penetrate
the mind.

Standing
bent
with unrestrainable
heart,

equally difficult,
sullen towards Death:
penetrate
the mind.

AGAINST SORROW

After Rilke's letters

No letter to atone for silence.
           In unison with me,
space untouched,
           angelic space.
Quiet lamps.

                    I am too full.
           How I reproach myself,
no longer remaining idle.

           I think of you.
                I have words—
a tree.

                    And the poor rain.

I am absorbed,
                altered internally.
A page
        crossed and criss-
            crossed out.
A future open.
              Infinite
hopelessness cured.

I go out a lot evenings
against the chaos of time.

The maple trees'
             fired leaves.

THE EXPLORER

For Jane Holding's first cast bronze

In this bronze, a female walks, no tortured Rodin but
Rather the great mother as wiry wisdom woman, primeval,
Striding to gather what she already knows.

Somewhere walking:
                no
                                  somewhere just to be

A word spoken:
                yes
                              perhaps, but also

thought advancing:
                equine
                        sinewy.

Through life's hollows a
                civic lesson:
                              the world's rudeness

does not matter—
                cannot—
                              for the eyes have it:

a world's view of
                splendor and demise
                              uttered inaudibly

as a walk
                through leaves:
                              an autumn sound

breaking
                making whole:
                              astonished at

all—
                by nothing
                              diminished.

PARACELSUS: CONCERNING THE IRIS IN THE VASE

When these varied colors you see,
Persevere. Constantly fan their flame
Until their purple petals consume your cloaked
Distances. The Luna moth will
Lay down her green shawl tonight,
Iridescently white, if you will
Praise this high perfection which
Heals all. Cleanses all.
Whoever always uses this Gilead
Prepares a long fixéd life
Without rust or bruised corruption.
An innocent making and unmaking—
The glass-blower's tincture—
Proving, in fire, the molten lump endures.

TOIL, A DIVINE COMMANDMENT

Sending my body out into the dirt looking
for wheat straw tied to a gospel singer's arm
I met an old woman whose
hair was glowworms and tobacco
She smelled so good I saw figs
ripening early on the bush
I laid my hoe down
singing songs a bullet
sings to a target
I bet my teeth against each turn in the road
An omen took to the wind
I became a scholar of sails
My hoe a wrist in the soil
finding the housekeeper of roots
humming speak to me
Speak
to me

THE MAN WHO
ATE BUTTERFLIES

For John Menapace

You wouldn't think
he would do such a
thing in public in
front of children or
even dogs who have
been known to eat
wasps (are always
embarrassed) But he
cannot stop himself
To imagine the sweet
nectar stolen by the
proboscis the cool
air between the wings
the colored dust   He
thinks "Turkish De-
light! Yum! Yum!"
Before you know it he
has grabbed the poor
thing and swallowed
He likes flowers and
so spends many after-
noons visiting gardens

THE POPPY SUITE

For Patricia Owens and Lorenzo Muti

One poppy
                Lonely field

Two poppies
                Murmured conversation

Field of poppies
                Red musics

※※※

When notes break from
        the red
poppies' purple throats

I remember life's petals

strewn on the ground

※※※

Collect corn poppies
in small muslin bags
suspended round the neck

Pack tightly in straw
Send off the same day
before they lose their stained-glass
red staccato

Use them for syrup
Use their seeds
Eat their ferny glaucous foliage
Hear their red music

                        ***

If you had seen the poppies there
in the half-shade summer's Tuileries

        you'd say

What bad luck to bloom
and fall
      so quickly
                  when
     night's music
     can swing so sweetly
above the hard clay

But, oh, what red music
                under the orange
sun
      and what
black throats to sing

                        ***

Shy goose-necked unopened buds
pressed and folded within

on May's bright morning
shaking out crumpled
solemn sounding
somber red musics

      ***

Poppies in a field

      Red music
cracking the crickets'
     ears

      ***

   A little night
       music?
You'd think the red

     poppy
had written it...

No matter what time

   of day
      a little night

sizzles in its red musics
      its black throat tremolo

JULY APPLES

My feet
           scorch on the path
A cool spring
           offers its water
The tingling
           goes deeper than skin
It shoots through
the bladder
           into the lungs
I become
        a blow-fish
        green-glistening
I go now
with sure-footed grace
           into the city
to a place
        I recognize
although I do not know
its sound
I can hold
back
no longer
        my hand's
        sparrow movement
        the continual coal
        burning
           inside my living

This tree
whose fruit
          opens a window
into the earth's old voice

OCTOBER SONG

Let whatever dies be
                    resurrected.
The cardinal waits in
the cedar branches
                    for a diamond,
      a snowflake,
                a spring memory
tremor, and then

flight, and then
autumn paisley fires
transmuted from
                  coarse to fine:

oblivion's path to the elemental
and back.
                  Before black earth
swallows all.   Last snap
of umber and rust.

THE RAISING OF LAZARUS

Lazarus, come forth
Jesus of Nazareth

A two-fold dying
and then
a two-fold life generated.

This earthly cabinet drawn
towards heat:
its own raw opposite.

The Judah hills return.
The locust tree beside
the cave.

Sparrows smudge
above astonished faces.
Out of that many,

the one
undying redness.
Him.

In the beginning,
a winding sheet.
Olive oil's green odor,

cold.
The infinite instrument,
blinding. And now

these supple
turbulent
thighs

kneeling down.

THE DREAM

They found him in the kitchen
The full moon
beside him with her braided hair
an empty kettle
four stones in a semicircle
on the table

They found a blue word on his tongue
onions in the basket with compasses ready
the frail canopy his blood
bathing his hands
his ten fingers crimped pages
in a book
yellowed
the compasses pointing True North

They found him with my face
and your lips at
the base of his jaw
They found him singing an old song
from the country of crones
about the woods he walked in
when he was young and downy
before he saw

I HAVE NEVER WANTED

I have never wanted to
                        write
    the perfect poem, only
the im
    perfect, as the human is
as the stone
        underfoot's not
    perfect
            but perfected by its being
stone:
      the poem
              perfected
by its being
        and me being
    human
            also that.

I have always wanted the
                        under
    side of things, the side
shaded
        by moss, the coolness under
the walkway
        stone, the silver and
    spotted
            backside of the *Elaeagnus*
leaf.

       I have
                always
wanted the elegance
                  of the unseen
     when the
                   light

first comes through and the shine
                                was
   (is) there all the time
wanted:

       I have
              always wanted

the poem
               perfected.

WINTER CEDARS

Know, my son, that that which is born of the Crow is the beginning of the Art.

—Hermes Trismegistus

The world must have come first—before the word. Did it—the world come first? And the glittering bits of disintegration shine at times. I don't know how to tell you or myself. I do know I want the detail (some slant memory and half-contented imagination) and the image, something like the orange in the hedge this day (October) and the three men working in the cemetery across the road from where these words go out to try to say what cannot ever be—the world is coming on so constantly.

—Shelby Stephenson

GHAZAL OF LAMENT

I store my words
in great piles of crusty

leaves.
Wait for them to bleat

to open and awaken me.
Enough to have them I tell myself.

Not sell them nor hold them up before
the others.

Sometimes over the ridges crows fly.
My words bluster in the wind

on autumn days.

MEDITATION ON THE DEATH OF A BIRD

At the feeders
two turtle doves
a cardinal
juncos

All too human
to think
a man
could know

A bird

LE QUATTRO STAGIONI

PRIMAVERA   SPRING

Time of illusive
shadblow:
white snow when
snow supposedly has turned
its back on the world.

Yellow time:
forsythia
and daffodil
the sun's tiger-green eyes
through new sycamore leaves.

The skink:
electric fellow
listening for the goldfinch
waiting for the ant's
civilized caravans to return.

Mothers
floating
up:
scent of violets
from ruined earth.

ESTATE   SUMMER

You would not believe it
if I told you
but I will tell you
anyway.

The light faded,
old fruit
darkened around its
edges.

Rains came pouring:
water from giants
in the sky to the giants
of the earth.

All laughing
at us, at each other,
laughing so hard
their tears cleansed

the still paths
in the garden—
the more still paths
in the soul.

AUTUMNO   FALL

In dry grasses—
crickets—
brothers to Orpheus.

Geese in pairs.
Their cowed heads
contented, wine-colored.

Late daisies—
fiddle music—
the goldenrod's torches.

A jig for love—
Love me—
Love me not—

Love me.

INVERNO   WINTER

Ice forms before we can name it,
although its name is as old as the world.
In the night white fires smolder,
our bodies heating the cold's corners.

Morning light:
squirrels waking to dig
snow.
Chickadees' slow

hammering.
Cardinals' sly crack
opening the chill.
Between snowflakes

the butterfly's heart.
Between snowflakes:
Silence.   The night sky.
A human voice remembering.

MONET

So there would be
                              flowers
to paint on rainy days
I planted
                    my kitchen garden
never knowing
the years would bring
                          this rain to my eyes
                          the Blue
When the rains come
                          as they do
I seem to know
                    the shortening days the
                yellow sound of
            birds
              both
                              muses in disquiet
Cobalt lilies bend
beneath the window
                then
                      the fringed
        peony
             opens
                    white
                              its final deluge
I want to watch them
                      hold them
apples to my mouth

THE LOOM

Willie Mae Gill
1903-1995

She lived for cotton,
the growth of sons,
one daughter lame, a mother
ornery, mean.
She walked with coleus,
gloxinia, begonia stems,
rooting in a well-dug humus from
the woods. Sung hymns,
washed pots, forgave.
Left nothing undone.
Molted in summer's tomato-scent air,
in winter took wings
warped by textile's shuttle.
No searing hardship, no
humidity, feared.
Not any fabric
weaves on any loom.

THE STROKE

For my Father

You can
        listen
                for hours and
not hear it:
the ragged
            body
spitting and whirring in
                half-time.
The soul's
apparent savagery
cutting cutting
its terrestrial web.

Mortality's
the last to go
after all the
slings
       and daggers.
The first
to grab hold.

Doesn't the heart
celebrate and buoy
the soul   or must it
always
     (as the hive
             finishes)
go? Death

                    puzzles
us so.
Not
the ragged dandelion
casting
            to the sun.

We've fed the old myths
to the dogs who
have no use for them.

OWL FLIGHT

This morning the world still
                         half-dark
an owl flew off near the house
into the woods
                         fast
     wings out-spread

       floating
                     free falling

Whoosh shook the dawn
                         Breakneck rose the sun

Alarm sweetened the terrorized rain
the tender-waking other birds
quick as match-flicks
                 condensed spheres of smoky twitter

       Royal owl

Cosmos in him
Dawn-wakener

               Thunder-stealer

THE CRAB KING

For Patricia Owens, Mary Frances Vogler, Stanley Finch
New Bern, Independence Day 1999

It's not greed
                      that demands I should catch you,

but the Goddess
                who decrees
                that we should eat,
                              that each of us
at one time, or another, under the silver sun
will give up the self so
                another might live.

You out-foxed me again and again—
sleazy pig tails
                sullying the water
with their salts,
                one feather floating above you
                offered as a barge.

What can I give you as fair exchange?

Eye for eye?
                Tooth for tooth? Or
simply praise-song in these words
                            which sacrifice, too,
                            sayeth the Lord,

as my body continues browning under summer's lamp,

and the light goes out in you,
                              entering me
                                              with atoning claws?

My promise? To live!
                                Live!

No longer crawling along the dirty-sanded bottom,
but up in the light,

                        where the skin peels.
                        Where the spirit has a house.

MOSS

Tenderly will I use your curling grass,
It may be you transpire from the breasts of young men.
Walt Whitman

If grass is earth's hair
then this is earth's
                        secret armpit and
           groin—
fleeced and feathered
where musk and dew

augur wind-blown shade

where maleness draws into dirt
                          and roots tingle
with animosity and grace

Forbidden adhesiveness and merge

        The hair of lovers

ALBINO DEER

How still he stands
among the rash scrubbery
down in the flat wet
below the roadbed.

Pink eyes fearless.
Tail flashless in
stockaded stillness.

He turns, ambling away,
slipping into the bare tree tangle.
White shard.
Sheeny brightness.

Gone.

***

Alain spots a deer:

Dear snow white deer,
in the middle of nowhere,
how did I find such a treasure?

Are you listening for
thank you letters?
For love?

***

Albino deer, farewell:

What did he leave?
What trail of almost goose
feathers impaled on the bushes?
A mind-candle, surely.
The pink underskin
of the world
radiant, fair.

ON WATCHING A STORM APPROACH

It will not elude me
stripped to skin

ribbed breast brushing against
sweet gum

cardinal chirping in the shrubbery.

The beetle lies in wait.
The worm craves its warm tunnels.

Rivulets seeking the merge
the torrent, the metaphor thunder.

Clouds down from
the Appalachians.

FOG

                comes fragrantly
across the mountain,
a golden dream
                        a luminous dream
filled with moths left struggling,
                    cut grass's
ragged smell
                      through the windows.

This is how peace comes:

silent and hard as gold
up through the cinders of the drive.

You are there in the crab apple's rotten
                        symphony,
there when I cry out
                  in the dream.

Perhaps you like us best then:

we disintegrate
          in order for your newness
your rawness
                  to manifest.

RISING

it seems
from under earth
dragging behind them vines and
moonlight

birds' songs breaking

small and without blemish

A SPELL FOR POEM-MAKING

A hunger grips my voice
I should not lay it low
Each member has its cry
And I   I move too slow

The rhythms of my heat
The shallows of my arm
Cicadas in sweat-filled air
Tremors of the farm

Confused and like a flame
Wobbling in a breeze
My fragrant voice becomes
A sibilant dis-ease

For everything that moves
I catch the very wind
Sunset in the dogwoods
Southern light within

Could everything but move
Into this steamy light
Provoke my voice its cherubim
Then I could waken night

The chancellor of words
The president of sound

THE EAST

No matter what your movements during the day, nor what face you leave uncovered at night under thick cottons and quiltings, or in summer when legs resemble beasts flailing in air, it is always there. You cannot turn away from it, nor drown, nor speak softly of stirrings in the abdomen or heart without sensing it—five-pointed, glittering from the depths of space in its irregular but pure orbit. Whiteness and gold. A sighing or unspeakable urge within the bones. It is the East—silence's great carrier singing, appearing on tops of mown hay, when final fruits are stored, and trees and all else green and growing drop their sleeves into the sharp violet sleeping cold. But it is there. A dwelling and warmth beside which no blast has power. In forgetful and fearful moments it turns to us—a constellation, a falcon soaring above cattle.

No matter. We cannot avoid it. It is the single clear portion in the wind. From it the promise comes.

A NEW USEFULNESS

Once, knowing fullness, the jar stored corn, tomatoes, pickles, and, for a short time, a bouquet of white daisies and pink cornflowers. But that is all past. It is always dark here, and some old images refuse to come forth. The jar does not hear the wind, nor feel boiling waters. However, there is breathing, or something like breathing, awakening it each morning when a few flecks of light enter the darkness.

The jar wonders if this breathing is the world or the absence of it; or if the world still exists, really, and if not, whether the cellar floats, uprooted in space.

Without sunlight, the jar becomes dark, tanned by dust and blackened by the cellar's loneliness. In the beginning it could see its reflection from all sides. Now, it sees only spiders and minute fields of damp earth settling on it. It looks empty, but it senses an accumulation of invisible beings, spirit-shapes that curl and multiply within the womb of its cold roundness.

Something about this jar betrays significance. It's possible that its shape, though pressed, repeats desire from the hand of the forge presser, for repetition is the mirror of need, and molten glass strives for perfection and finishing. Perhaps it holds some secret yet greater than molecules or amoeba. Esoteric knowledge lives in strange vessels, oftentimes common. The jar knows from experience, for example, secrets are carried in the bosom of the beet, and praise in the melon's seed. Now, the absinthe of storing is in the basics of living: a coating of damp dust, a spider's silvered weavings, a light, golden viscosity.

Here, things are heavy, yet always transforming. The jar's metamorphosis has begun, mineral-encrusted, making for a new life where being held by emptiness fulfills all needs. "My, my," it thinks, "a new and solitary usefulness."

CITYSCAPE

For Tunney Cobb, Pat Woods, and Stanley Finch

Barrenness, not sterility,
abides. Here
the alleyway stretches from
the hotel window
to the hilltop where
the punctuated view
narrows by rust and
brick.
Sky, March gray.
Buildings gray, stucco,

off-white, pale blue.
At the end,
pigeons, made small,
scatter. But
closer, near
where the squirrel plays
in the cool morning,
cherry petals
shatter

in the breeze—pink
snow
on the pavement.

Delicate and light,
going
some
where
even the eye
longs for. Away

from here.

FROM A TRAIN AT DUSK SOMEWHERE IN VIRGINIA

The armadillos of the sun
make trees into pheasants

Shetlands graze
A cold wind stills the evening

My body sweetens
My spirit's darkened roosters crow

PERSIMMON

For Robert Bell

For about fifty feet above me the straight trunk rises with its scaly square bark. This edge of the field has already turned brown. The first frost and a short autumn rain last week made sure of that. All color has taken to air, splattering the nearby woods with yellow, gold, and ruddy red. Some people call this tree "possumwood" because our nocturnal friend so fondly sleeps in its branches. It's commonly called "persimmon," an old Algonquian name.* Its leaves fell earlier.

The limbs splay out, mad and snaky. The sun sinks behind it, and from my footing in the field, it seems a thousand Chinese lanterns light up. "Fruit of the Gods" the Indians called it. Only the virtuous could eat such clean, orange fruit—a defenseless layer of earth's cool breath dusting its flesh. Only a possum dare sleep in such branches.

The loveless have friends in fields with persimmons at the edges, where all loss gathers in burly branches shot through with a natural sorrow. My friend, grandchild of an Indian and a Black, nothing so bleak as bare trees will do for you; but this one, whose laden fruit, warmly colored, sour before frost, wrought with poison, is sweet to the mouth now. The year in ruin. A field never before known. Trembling in silence.

---

* *Putchamin, pasiminan,* or *pessamin,* from the Algonquian Powhatan

A PAUSE FOR CELEBRATION

For Alice Faulkner

The peerless grasshopper waits
among mint and snap
                       dragons.
He searches for his song.
Finally, it comes.

ALZARI COL SOLE
(TO RISE WITH THE SUN)

Salute, *a song for Alice Welsh*

Oh you would be amazed to know
what places I have been what
stairways I have climbed what
doors have shut behind me what
birds and where and when they sang
If only you could smell the hot slumber
of cardamom and jasmine rice
of olive groves on hills or
rain coming across the plains
hair tonic mastering the unruly hair of men
magnolias soughing through summer windows
Oh you would be amazed at what
stories I've told what stories I've heard
what stories I have forgotten what
stories I wish I did not know
It would amaze you my friends what
tables I have laid and risen from what
wines tasted what dishes devoured what
beds rumpled and possessed Oh
you would be amazed by crossroads
where we have met each other unknown
toasted and warmed to each other
praising the awkward wisdoms of living
living the praise-tasting clementines
each slice held faultlessly to the mouth a
word murmured under shade trees

in this simmering south of our age
amazed by cool shadows while the past
dazzles the day's eye the simple tangle
of our remembered ways the prodigious sun

NATTY KATHMANDU DREADS, PRINCESS NATULLAH, NINA, NAT, PRISSY, NANNY, NANA, NEEN-NEE, HEADWALKER: IN MEMORIAM

March 1980-March 14, 1995

A Death in the house today:
unexpected, grim, our hearts
spinning on spidery strings.
You would have liked that,
trim as you were,
eagerly black, eagerly always
after the strange.

A Death in the house today:
paws now silent
on the stairs,
instead of shadow chasing, or
dipping feet into the water bowl
before a drink. Splashing
in rhythm.

A Death in the house today:
constant conversation ceased,
or continued, perhaps, at your ease,
past our hearing,
with other cat ghosts.
No more your innocent
frenzy. Your fresh look.

The house bereft of you.
The string spinning.
A Death in the house today.
Your Death, yours,
O Bright Cat, O Scholar of
Accidents, O Green-eyed
Manic Mirth!

KALI, KATIE MICKIE, GIRTHA KITTY FATTIE LABELLE, QUEEN KALIM, ROUNDBALL, OUR KATE: IN MEMORIAM

March 1980-January 25, 1994

Your fur was rich.
Your motions always fine.
Your startled owl eyes
never questioned ours.

Your girth inspired wide
oceans of praise,
amazement at your delicate
(and indelicate)

grooming ways.
Ballet forged
by feline counterpoint.
Gravity dismayed.

Silent daughter.
Rabbit furred nobility.
At home in wood and garden,
field and chair.

Now separate and incorporeal.
Still loved. Now still.

SCORPION

The scorpion on the ledge
does not know what I know

The scorpion on the ledge
has a knife and hole

The scorpion of the ledge
pledges indifference

The scorpion on the ledge
protects from all sorrows

SHADOW

Dear one who lists
me among your treasures

Your shoulders' shy turning
says the gate opens

closes
I am welcome

The path knows your footsteps
When you go out blue

jays rage in judges' coats
You tap your foot

hair stands on end
To fall into you

is to hear rifles
crying

for the heart

DOG SLEEPING

For Lord Dewitt Dogmeat Bodhisattva

He sleeps the rugged deep sleep
that knows sleep as a rest and letting go
after the rock escarpment
climax of a climb—
the flightless sound birds make when
dirt bathes their parasitic skins—
the sleep that stills (a log they say)
yet gathers strength in
each extremity to twitch
with dreams from air. The
sleep that mothers wish for
and fear in night's illness.

It comes so easily to him,
a scalawag, a mentor, and
a beast. It rises rhythmically
near his loins. And when through soft
and furry breath
sufficiently care dissipates,
the Lord Dog rises,
bows nobly to the sun, his charioteer,
and goes, off to the next mountain,
or gully, or pond just as humans do,
as around each turn
they find their unexpected life.

CAT POETRY

The Voice should never be separated from the Utterance.
The Zohar

In Poetry, I
have no use for cats. If I am steady,
they are roly-poly. If
I am sleek, their fur flies.
When I am incessant, the cats
recline, soft stones,
conversant with the earth.
When I am talkative, they hold their
peace, they say nothing except
what must, what has, to be said.
What has this to do with Poetry. Or Song?
Oh no, in Poetry, I have no use
for cats. I have three names,
while their names multiply,
(limp mice for catching),
names elaborate and bold, mutable
and unflappable, etched even,
flexible as fence-walker's
names must be. I have no use
for cats. Cats ellipse, cats rarefy
the obvious. Mirror the world
and rule it. Make fantasy.
What has this to do with Poetry, or
Song? Cats have claws, while words
can only prick. Cats have wisdom,
courage. Are slick. Are static
and ecstatic. Can poems be so?

I have no use for cats. In Poetry
I mean. Oh, No! Never. Such
inconstant constancy could find no
place there, do you think?
A limber back bone and supple
landing could never do in poems.
They have no temper, only tone.
(Or do they?) I have no use
for them. They are too...
comfortable. Their colors too
imaginable. They are beasts for children,
not Gods for mummification
in poetic tombs. (Or are they?)
Fit for nursery rhymes, surely,
but not eternity's vellum. (Ah, vellum,
such a cushy, purring word.) Why
cats eat birds and mice and...
and shrews! What kind of meal
is that? Is Poetry
wild or primitive,
bloodthirsty, cruel,
fickle, or too kind?
I've never known a poem
to scroll lovingly
around your legs. Have
you? In Poetry, surely,
there is no use for cats.

IN PROVENCE

For Jack Fullilove and Alain LeSage

After miles of bare trees
and cypresses

what's this

a spindly shock
canary yellow

A tree twelve feet tall
grappling out
of a walled garden

Leaves
        flames
citron-colored

The world keeping
secrets from me
then this

LUNCH

Though winter
           sticks in the country's
                        heart
plum trees
       bloom in Valence.
                     The boy on the train
has his magazines,
          his music, his dreams.
                         His mother
nurses her sandwich:
           dry bread and
                    polished meat, a simple
lunch.
     Though winter blooms
               in Valence, the mother
languishes:
      her youth used up.
                   Her son cloaks
grey eyes
      under her gaze,
              waiting for some-
thing to chew on.
      Taste.
                 Something blooming
which he cannot name.

IN LUCCA

Sweet angel, little Italian boy,
whose voice rises with his mother's
in the afternoon light and the old woman
crooning to her cat in the courtyard's shadow,
the pigeons' cooing, the piano
melancholy from an upstairs room,
this beautiful sameness greeting us each afternoon
as the day descends in the churches,
in the old town, and the Madonna,
San Sebastiano, San Michele,
flutter above the roof tiles,
their haloes, arrows, wings
trembling secretly, phrases
repeated over and over by the child,
and the room settling into soothing
monotony, and the sunset, and the sweet
angel Italian child waiting
impatiently for his supper to come.

PARNASSUS, THE BARREN CLEFT

For Jonathan Williams, after Andrew Young

We should
        of course
                be grateful
from such an elevation—
            distracted
                    by some plant—
saxifrage
      among the rocks
             urging us on:
after the wind—
        a still small
              voice
The clouds—
        tired—
              hang low to the hills
In them
      a tempting brightness
                  making us short-sighted
god-like
      Mountains
            smoking
on all sides
      Pastures below—
                a steaming cauldron
The earth on fire

     The river
          a serpent winding
from wet fire
    Our eyes
        trespassed
to dim distance

     Above all
         the mountain
huger than itself

WINTER CEDARS

These solitary things—
                          wretched statues
            fragments
                    of the waxing moon

For all this to happen
                              becoming landscape
myself

                my mouth

in prayer
                    To attach myself

ghostly   terrible

                              to the tall cedars

Teaching Daylilies How to Read

A few years ago I submitted work to a Southern lit magazine, *The Dead Mule*, which requires in fun, as part of the submission process, that the writer include a statement of Southern legitimacy. I've expanded it a bit, and also, in fun, include it as a postscript to *The Broken Flower*.

I was born and raised in the feudal mill village of Kannapolis, North Carolina, in the 1950's, have never lived outside the state, and don't want to. When I was a child my neighbor Preacher Pethel ran a country store, plowed everyone's Victory Garden with a mule during the week, and preached Hell-fire on the weekends. I sang hymns with his granddaughter many a Saturday and Sunday night and learned how to hold a note until the bees swarmed. One day when a black snake slithered down the hill toward my grandma and me hoeing in her garden up the street from my house, the Preacher and every other grown man in the neighborhood appeared with their Personal Hoe to take on that critter. After seeing it hang on a fence post for a week I knew I'd love snakes the rest of my life.

I was born knowing the difference between Eastern and Western North Carolinians, and Eastern and Western North Carolina barbecue [both noun and verb]. Of Appalachian Scots-Irish and Cherokee stock (with some Pennsylvania-Dutch thrown in to sweeten the ball, not flat, dumplings), one would think I would prefer Lexington-stylecue, but I don't, even though it's just fine, especially with that red slaw; rather give me some Wilson, North Carolina barbecue, yellow slaw, and corn sticks anytime [although, in truth, the best cue anywhere, except in Umbria, Italy, is at Allen & Sons in Chapel Hill with the white slaw I most prefer]. I'm born redneck and White Trash, and bred-in-the-bone Yallah Dawg Democrat, which I reckon has something to do with being descended from a refugee Calvinist preacher and his exiled Hapsburg princess wife.

Having been Eastern Indian in my last life, I embrace Vedanta and Jesus [the real one not the current day self-righteous one], and given a choice between my fantasy desert island meal of country style steak, lima beans, sweet potato biscuits, and Grandma Gill's pound cake or Goa Fish Curry, onion chutney, paratha, and raita, I'd have it all and ask for more. Luckily okra comes compliments of both cultures. In addition, I'll have a glass each, just to display my New South cosmic-cosmopolitan taste, of some black wine of Cahor, Sicilian Nero d'Avola, Provençal amber-colored Rosé, Prosecco, Veuve Clicquot, and French Suze. Then a thimble-full each of Nocello, Limoncello (homemade please), Siennese Amaro, and Lot Valley Pruneau (also, homemade please). Maybe I'm not Southern enough, but I just can't drink bourbon. One strike against me, I know, but you'll like me after I've downed all that fancy southern European stuff. Wait … please throw in some English bitters—a pint will do.

If that's not enough to get your Mule ears listening, then let me tell you that I eat banana sandwiches (sometimes with peanut butter in addition to the Duke's mayonnaise), fried chicken, chicken livers (Dip's please), devilled eggs, okra, and collards—and drink sweet tea with abandon. Being Southern, I am full of lovely loving contradictions and thus hate white grits which to my taste should only be eaten as a condiment for pools of butter; but I adore yellow grits, and stone or water ground grits with runny eggs glazing through. Those yellow grits? We didn't eat grits for breakfast; we had corn meal mush with red-eye gravy. Thus when I first crossed the Ponte Vecchio I realized, Southern as I am, that I was also Italian. Another former life? Or the next one; I don't know.

I wish I had the gumption to be vegetarian, but oh I do so love hawg, and I think plants have just as much soul as we animals, so what's up with that? Oh, and Neese's sausage is just great, especially the extra sage. But beware of Neese's Liver Pudding in Blowing Rock which I grew up devouring, and Tom Thumb (also known as

Thingamajig) from the Wilson County area. As my father would say "Pretty good eat'n for the poor!"

I think kudzu in flower is one of the earth's greatest pleasures, and goldenrod and sumac the most beautiful doorways into the corridors of coming winter. Trees. Oh, how I love trees. I could eat'm with a spoon. That's not allowed, but persimmons are. Now that's a puddin' to write home about, and Jane knows how to make it. Two spiritual guides, one Southern, one Japanese, speak to trees better than anyone: Ms. Welty declared, "How can you go out on a limb if you don't know your own?" While that Eastern dude Musō Soseki advised, "Don't ask why the pine trees/in the front garden/are gnarled and crooked// The straightness/they were born with/is right there inside them." I trust my poems smell of pine and chrysanthemums, cut grass and cedar posts, and that the crookedness in them shows I know the limb I'm hanging on. I wrote my first poems high up in the fork of a *Mimosa*; a fragrance never forgotten.

Some folks might not consider most of my work Southern enough, but I do. It don't matter to me. My vale of humility has room enough for another's mountain of conceit. Without the slightest hesitation I'd sleep on a bed of moss with ticks and beetles to hear the earth sing. A blue mountain all smoked up is the most erotic sight I ever did see. Now I'm not saying those roiling waves on the Banks don't do it to me too—they do. If you gonna have one contradiction you might as well have a thousand. "*Magnolia, Camellia, Gardenia* thrall." That's the refrain.

But listen to this. My Scots-Irish and Cherokee bloods allows me visions and to believe'm, no matter how the practical Calvinist and Pennsylvania-Dutch fire in the veins might fight against it. I see all kinds of beings in the blesséd outdoors and next to the hearth without a whimper or a scare. I've parleyed with fairies and leprechauns many a time and no one will ever convince me otherwise. I even woke up once to a goblin creeping into my bed. One swift kick and he was gone. I'm legitimately Southern and proud of it which makes me ordinary and strange at the same time.

Jonathan Williams once told me that we needed to teach daylilies how to read and so, ever since then, that's what I've been trying to do.

Golgonooza at Frog Level
June, 2012

ACKNOWLEDGEMENTS

Some of these poems have appeared in the following publications—grateful acknowledgement is here made:

Alpha Beat Press Chaplet Series, *The Arts Journal, The Asheville Poetry Review, The Asheville Poetry Review Tenth Anniversary Anthology, Assaracus, Big Bridge, Blue Buildings, Caesura, The Carolina Quarterly, Chapel Hill News, The Dead Mule, Double Dealer Redux, Dreamworks, Earth and Soul: An Anthology of North Carolina Poetry* (Kostroma Writers Organization, Russia), *Frank* (Paris), *The Front Page, Gay City Anthologies* (Volumes One and Two), Green Finch Keenings broadsides, *Hummingbird, The Independent Weekly, Iris: The UNC Journal of Medicine,* The Jargon Society web site *Musings for the Season, Light and Shadow: The Photographs of Claire Yaffa* (Aperture), *Listen Magazine for UNC-CH Public Radio, Literary Trails of the North Carolina Piedmont, Main Street Rag, MsManagement: Newsletter of the North Carolina Library Association Roundtable on the Status of Women in Librarianship, A Murder of Crows, My Laureate's Lasso* (North Carolina Poet Laureate Kay Byer's blog Poet of the Week feature), *Negative Capability, The News and Observer, North Carolina Literary Review, North Carolina Poets on 9/11,* North Carolina Wesleyan College Press Visiting Writers Broadside Series, *On Hounded Ground: Home and the Creative Life* (an essay with poems) (Bookgirl Press, Sendai, Japan), Bards on the Bus project (*The Carolina Quarterly* and the Chapel Hill Transit System), *Oyster Boy Review, Pembroke Magazine, Pen and Brush: A Collection of the Best Illustrations and Their Poems from Hummingbird's First Fifteen Years, Poetry Now, Poetry Salzburg Review, The Prose Poem, The Quality of Life* by Janet Lembke (Lyons Press), *qarrtsiluni, Saint John's Review, The Simple Vows Anthology, Sparks of Fire: Blake in a New Age Anthology* (North Atlantic Books), *Success! One: Chimera* (I am my own twin), *Word and Witness: 100 Years of North Carolina Poetry* (Carolina Academic Press), *The Sun, The Symposium,* University of North Carolina Library Manuscript Collection's WEBsite virtual poems, *University of North Carolina Library Staff Newsletter, Wolfpen Branch, The Worcester Review,* and the Yellow Pepper Press broadside series.

A number of these poems were displayed as part of two photography exhibits *Daedalus Landed Here: Poetic Views—Earthly Travels* (October-November 2006), and *Not What It Seems* (April-June 2010) at Through This Lens Gallery in Durham, North Carolina. Thank you Roylee "Duvie" Duvall—my best friend in junior high, high school and college—for reappearing in my life and encouraging my different eye.

To all the bookstores, libraries, universities, schools, theaters, churches, homes, and other organizations that have given me an oral proving ground for these poems: "Praise is the practice of art" William Blake. A special thanks to Ann Barlow for commissioning *Le Quattro Stagioni,* and to Patricia Owens (Chamber Orchestra of the Triangle) for commissioning *The Poppy Suite.*

Many of these poems appear on *What We Have Lost: New and Selected Poems 1977-2001* by Jeffery Beam available as a 2 CD set from Green Finch Press.

Thanks to Elizabeth Matheson for the cover image.

The author would like to express his appreciation to the Orange and Durham County Arts Councils whose support assisted in the writing of some of the poems in this manuscript.

As always, my deepest gratitude to Sam Ward for Skysill Press.

ALSO BY JEFFERY BEAM

The Golden Legend (Floating Island Publications)

Two Preludes for the Beautiful (Universal)

Midwinter Fires (French Broad Press)

The Fountain (NC Wesleyan College Press)

Submergences (Off the Cuff Books)

Light and Shadow: The Photographs of Claire Yaffa (Aperture)

little (diminishing books/Green Finch Press)

Visions of Dame Kind (The Jargon Society)

An Elizabethan Bestiary: Retold (Horse and Buggy Press)

What We Have Lost: New and Selected Poems 1977-2001
(Green Finch Press) [A spoken word/multimedia 2 CD collection]

Life of the Bee (Rock Valley Music)
[Libretto for a song cycle by Lee Hoiby]

*New Growth—Shauna Holiman and Friends:
New Songs and Spoken Poems* (Albany Records)
[A CD collection including Life of the Bee]

Lullaby of the Farm
[Illustrated chaplet to celebrate ten years of Winter Stories]

Old Sunflower, You Bowed to No One:
Poet Lorine Niedecker [Special supplement to *Oyster Boy Review*]

Gospel Earth and *Gospel Earth II*
(Longhouse Publishers and Booksellers)
[Two chaplet selections and an online chapbook]

On Hounded Ground: Home and the Creative Life
(Bookgirl Press, Japan)

The Beautiful Tendons:
Uncollected Queer Poems 1969-2007 (White Crane Books)

A Hornet's Nest (The Jargon Society/Green Finch Press)
[compiler/editor—a Jonathan Williams quote book]

Heaven's Birds: Lament and Song
[Libretto for a cantata by Steven Serpa]

An Invocation (Country Valley Press) [Limited edition chapbook]

The Lord of Orchards: Jonathan Williams at 80
[Online feature *Jacket* magazine—co-edited with Richard Owens]

Gospel Earth (Skysill Press)

Me Moving
(Longhouse Publishers and Booksellers)
[chaplet]

MountSeaEden (Chester Creek Press)
[Letterpress limited edition]

Midwinter Fires
(Seven Kitchens Press Rebound Series)
[A new edition with a new introduction by Joe Donahue]

The New Beautiful Tendons: Collected Queer Poems 1969–2012
(Spuyten Duyvil/Triton Books)

Blue Darter—Jonathan Williams:
A Bibliography of the Publications and Ephemera 1950-2008
[In Progress]

Family Secrets
A Jake Heggie song-cycle for soprano Andrea Moore
with Allan Gurganus, Randall Kenan, Michael Malone,
Frances Mayes, Lee Smith, Daniel Wallace
[In Progress]

Six Metamorphoses after Britten's Ovid
[In Progress—Libretto for Steven Serpa]

Ragnarök: He of Fire
[Erasure of Ignatius Donnelly's
The Destruction of Atlantis:
Ragnarök: The Age of Fire and Gravel]
[In Progress]

PRAISE FOR *THE BROKEN FLOWER*

The poems in Jeffery Beam's *The Broken Flower* call out to be shared. They make the reader want to exclaim to anyone nearby, "Here, read this! Relish this image. Savor these memorable lines: 'This tree / whose fruit / opens a window / into the earth's old voice.'" The earth's old voice is everywhere in these poems. Like windows opening, Beam's music calls us to come here. Like a tendril of honeysuckle, both delicate and durable, his poems unfold on the page. They bring to their readers, in the sheaf of this beautifully crafted book, nothing less than a gift.

—Kathryn Stripling Byer

The oblique poems in *The Broken Flower* (as Emily says: 'Tell all the Truth but tell it slant') circle around the heart of the matter. Jeffery Beam zones in, searching to decode mysteries 'to say / what is between.' And he discovers such rare moments as 'The skink: / electric fellow / listening for the goldfinch / waiting for the ant's / civilized caravans to return.'

—Jonathan Greene

Jeffery Beam's newest collection of poems, *The Broken Flower*, invites the reader to enter Beam's world through Smoky Mountain mists parting to reveal the 'dearest freshness deep down things.' Resisting every attempt to exhaust the crucial work of naming, *The Broken Flower* is the power of words to disrobe, to run and rest, to float on icy streams, to hang sere and healing in hot Appalachian barns. These poems return the reader to a true Eden, one both redeemed and fallen; the only possible Paradise where the first breath could have uttered the first word. *The Broken Flower* is testament and legacy to that breathing word and its lasting generation.

—Brian Zimmer

A true Southern Gentleman, Jeffrey Beam's quietly moving, spiritual and deeply human poems in *The Broken Flower* succeed in their attempt 'to say what is / between.' Whether looking at the world around him or contemplating works of art, Beam's explorations of the connection between man and nature, art and life, body and soul helps us to find beauty, joy, and meaning both within ourselves and 'In the discarded / shattered world.' I am grateful for the life-affirming vision of these finely crafted poems.

—Reginald Harris

Photo © 2009 Ted Pope

Jeffery Beam's many award-winning works include *Gospel Earth, Visions of Dame Kind, An Elizabethan Bestiary: Retold, Midwinter Fires, The Fountain*, and *The Beautiful Tendons: Uncollected Queer Poems 1969-2007*. His spoken word CD with multimedia, *What We Have Lost: New and Selected Poems 1977-2001*, was a 2003 Audio Publishers Award finalist. *The Lord of Orchard: Jonathan Williams at Eighty*—an online feature (with Richard Owens) for *Jacket* magazine—was published in 2009. The song cycle, *Life of the Bee*, with composer Lee Hoiby, continues to be performed on the international stage. The Carnegie Hall premiere, with Beam reading and the songs performed, can be heard on Albany Record's *New Growth*. His book-length surrealist gay-themed prose poem, *Submergences*, originally published as a chapbook in 1997 was reprinted in 2008 in Rebel Satori Press's *Madder Love: Queer Men and the Precincts of Surrealism*. On December 1, 2008 (World AIDS Day) in Boston, MA, composer/countertenor Steven Serpa premiered a cantata *Heaven's Birds: Lament and Song* based on three of Beam's poems from *The Beautiful Tendons*. Beam's poems and criticism have appeared in many anthologies and magazines.

Beam continues to work on the poetry collection *The Life of the Bee*, an opera libretto based on the Demeter/Persephone myth, a song cycle inspired by Benjamin Britten's *Six Metamorphoses after Ovid* with composer Steven Serpa, an erasure poem sequence based on Ignatius Donnelly's The *Destruction of Atlantis: Ragnarök: The Age of Fire and Gravel*, and a commonplace book on poetry and the spirit entitled *They Say*. He is also working with soprano Andrea Moore, composer Jake Heggie, and authors Allan Gurganus, Frances Mayes, Michael Malone, Lee Smith, and Daniel Wallace on a new song cycle, situated in Hillsborough, North Carolina, tentatively entitled *Family Secrets*. A chapbook collection, *Gilgamesh/Enkidu*, seeks a publisher. Forthcoming works include a book version of *The Lord of Orchards* and *Blue Darter—Jonathan Williams: A Bibliography of the Publications and Ephemera, 1950-2008*. *The New Beautiful Tendons: Collected Queer Poems 1969-2012* is published this year by Spuyten Duyvil/Triton Books. Beam retired in late 2011 from many decades as a botanical librarian UNC-Chapel Hill, North Carolina. He lives in Hillsborough, North Carolina with his partner of 33 years, Stanley Finch. You can read and hear more of his poetry at his website: www.unc.edu/~jeffbeam/index.html

www.ingramcontent.com/pod-product-compliance
Lightning Source LLC
Chambersburg PA
CBHW032127090426
42743CB00007B/491